BIRMINGHAM IN PHOTOGRAPHS

A Changing City

DAVE JENNINGS

AMBERLEY

First published 2020

Amberley Publishing
The Hill, Stroud
Gloucestershire, GL5 4EP

www.amberley-books.com

ISBN 978 1 4456 9670 6 (print)
ISBN 978 1 4456 9671 3 (ebook)

British Library Cataloguing in Publication Data.
A catalogue record for this book is available from the British Library.

Typesetting by Aura Technology and Software Services, India.
Printed in the UK.

INTRODUCTION

In this book I have tried to cover both the old and the new Birmingham, along with where the two combine. Even in the time it took to take these photographs, Birmingham has changed so much.

I would like to thank my girlfriend Sharon for joining me on a lot of my walks along the streets and canals of Birmingham, and for pointing out things I would have missed as I was looking in the wrong direction. I would also like to thank Amberley Publishing for trusting me with another book.

Looking from the Old Main Line Canal towards Hyatt Regency

Centenary Square

The Cube

Birmingham coach station, Digbeth, with the city skyline beyond

Corner of Well Street and Great Hampton Street, the Jewellery Quarter

Tramline terminal, Stephenson Street

Looking towards the Rotunda from New Street station

The Rest House, Bournville Green

The Old Fire Station, Lancaster Place, now student accommodation

River Rea, Digbeth

Grand Central

View from Grand Central towards the city centre

Graffiti at the Custard Factory

Telsen building, formerly Telsen Electrical Company

Birmingham City Council

Bullring market looking towards the city centre

Moor Street station

The Malt House

The old of Digbeth with the newer buildings of the city centre beyond

Centenary Square redevelopment

Birmingham back-to-backs, Hurst Street

Bridge from car park to Selfridges

Gasworks, Windsor Street

Moored-up narrowboats

Belmont Row

Gospel Street

Fort Dunlop – once home to tyre manufacturing, now office and retail space

Hyatt Regency from Birmingham Library

St Martin

Piccadilly Arcade

Graffiti, Custard Factory

Bullring market

Regent Row, Jewellery Quarter

Canal tunnel under Jennens Road

Looking back from the canal towards Cardigan Street

EST 2016
CLINK
BEER
Chitty's
cakes
limited
DEVIALET
PHANTOM

Gibb Street

Gibb Street

The Canal House

Tyseley station

The Jewellers Arms, Jewellery Quarter

Looking over Moor Street station

The Cube

The Electric Cinema, Station Street

Centenary Square

New Street station reflections

Redevelopment of the old
Birmingham Central Library

Site of Birmingham markets, now cleared for redevelopment

The Custard Factory, Digbeth

Looking across Cadbury Men's Recreation Grounds, Bournville

Cadbury offices, Bournville Place

Grand Central

Graffiti, Custard Factory

Gibb Street

The Jewellery Quarter

The Canal House

Modern Birmingham skyline

Tram travelling along Corporation Street

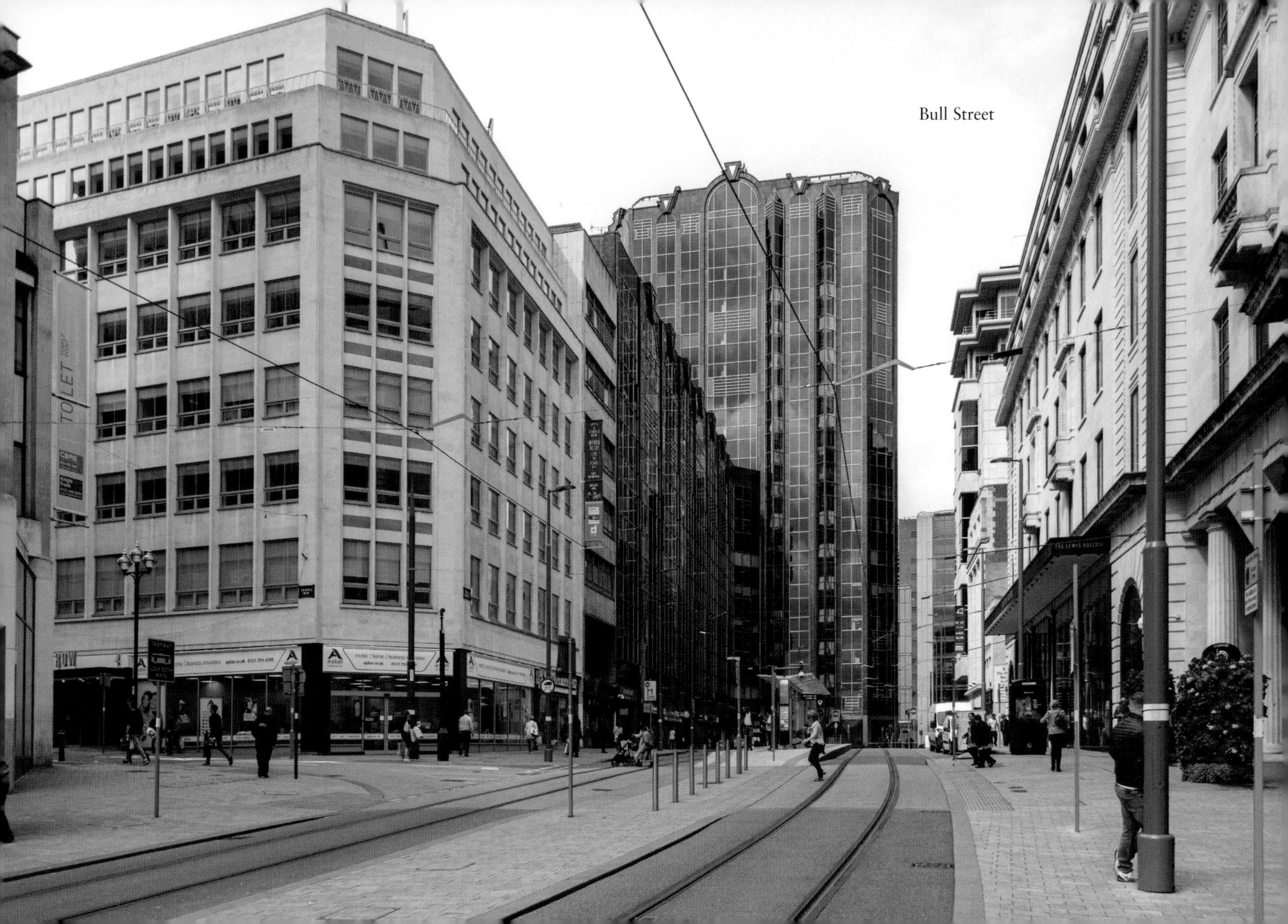
TO LET
motor | home | business insurance

Bull Street

Tram travelling along Corporation Street

City centre

View from Digbeth towards the city

The Argent Centre, Frederick Street

Birmingham Library appearing from above the concrete of the car park

Corner of Church Street and Edmund Street

Victoria Works, Jewllery Quarter, originally used for the manufacture of pen nibs

City skyline, with Birmighma Library to the right and modern apartments to the left

Cannon Street

Graffiti, Custard Factory

Canal behind National College for
Advanced Transport & Infrastructure

View along Edmund Street

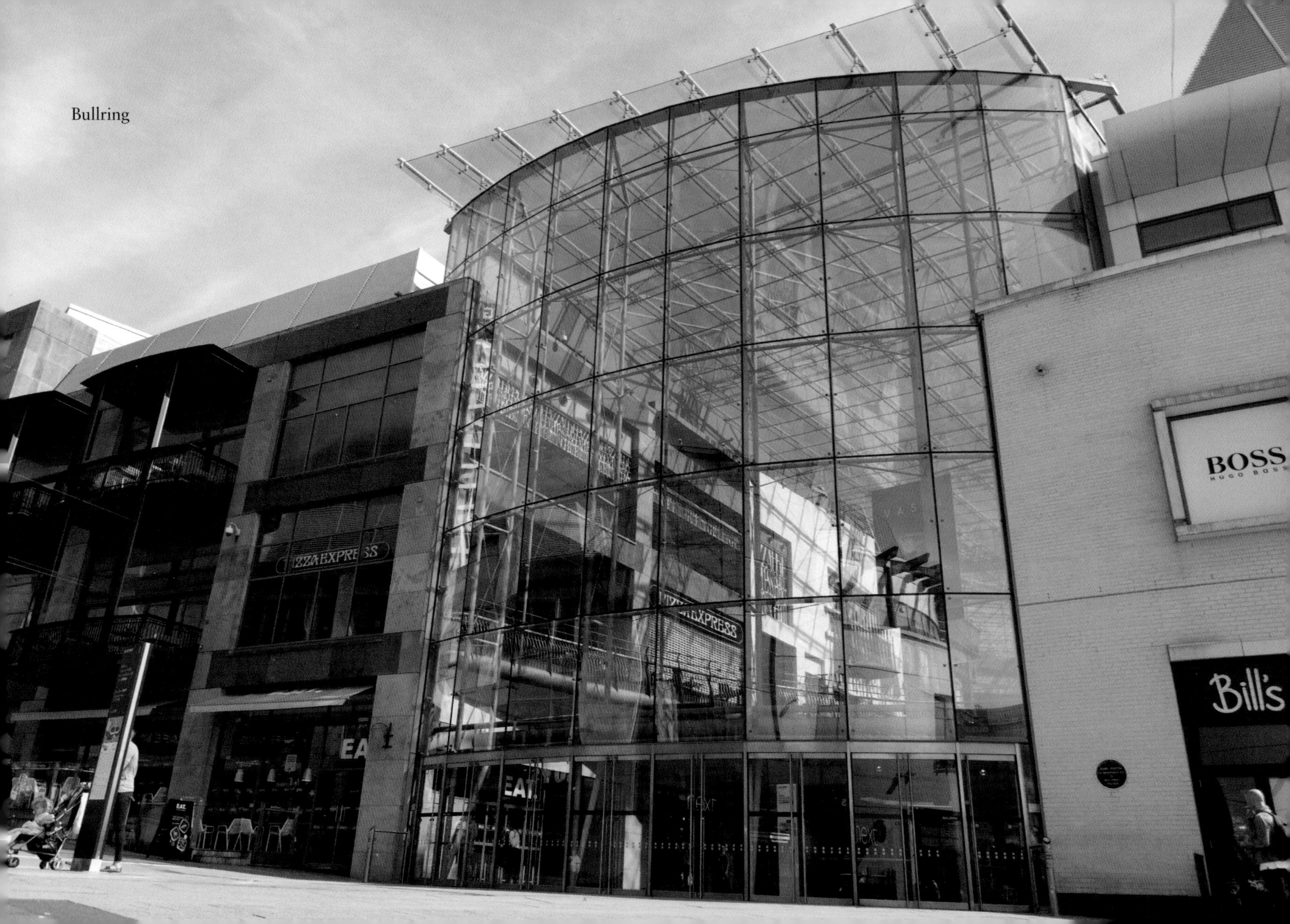
BOSS
HUGO BOSS
Bill's
EAT

Bullring

Rear Street

Warstone Lane, Jewellery Quarter

Redevelopment of what was once Birmingham Central Library

The Wharf

HSBC and Hyatt Regency

Selfridges

Canal towpath

View along Jennens Road back towards the city centre

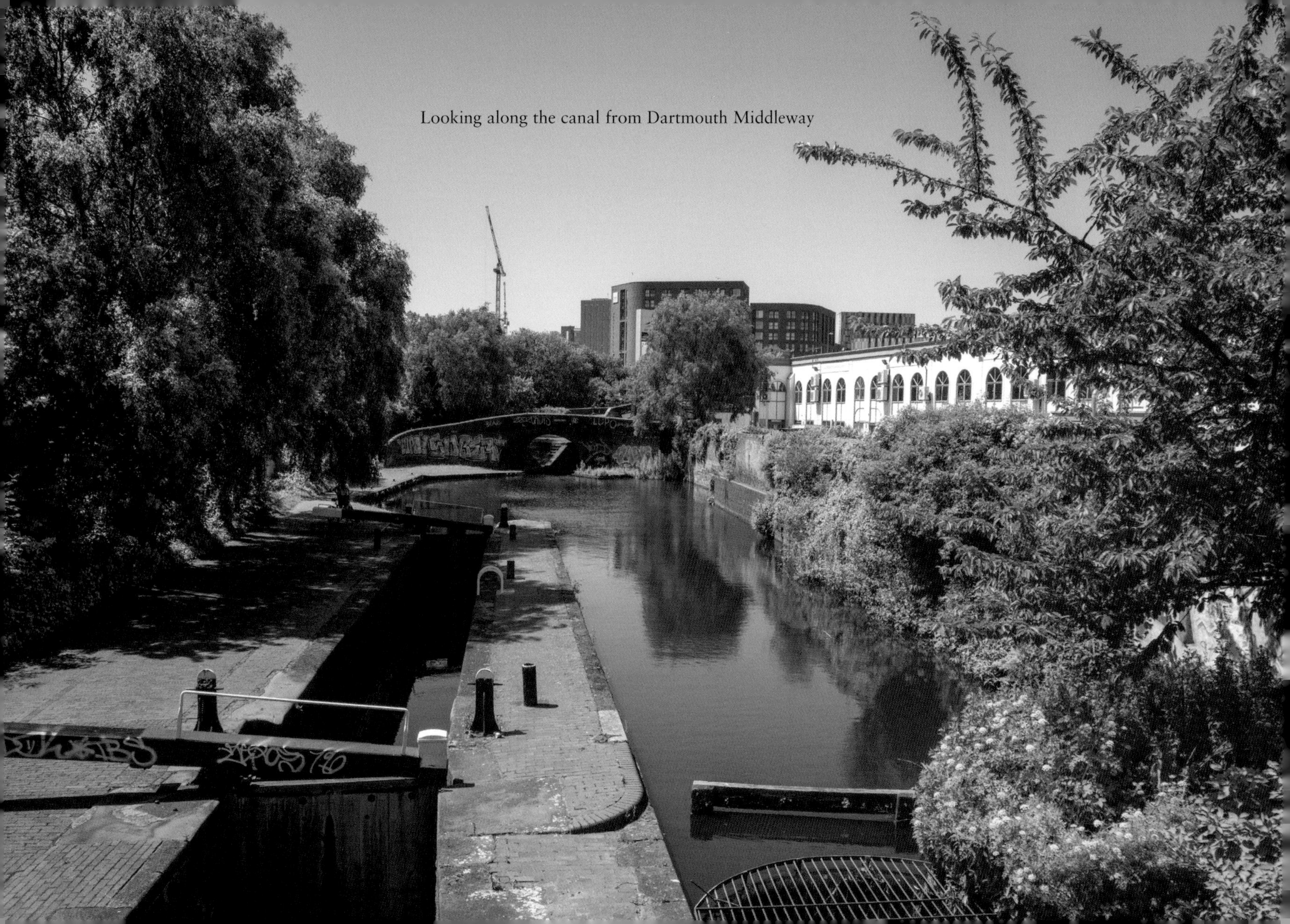

Looking along the canal from Dartmouth Middleway

Victoria Square

Derelict factory with Belmont Row in the background

The Radisson

New Street station

James Watt's beam engine, Dartmouth Circus

Birmingham Central Hall

Fazeley Street

Smallbrook Queensway

Grand Central with the Odeon beyond

Reflections in Grand Central

St Martin and Selfridges

City skyline from Bristol Street

Dartmouth Circus underpass

Centenary Square

Lakeside residencies

Birmingham Library

The Bullring

Chamberlain Square

View from Fort Dunlop looking back towards the M6

View from Colmore Queensway

Thomas Fattorini Ltd

Edgbaston Street

Stephenson Street

Stephenson Street

Old buildings of Digbeth with the more modern of the city in the distance

Canal graffiti

View from the Parade towards
Islington Gates and the BT Tower

Arena Birmingham and Sea Life Centre

The Distillery

Canal locks working their way up to Arena Birmingham

Selfridges at night

Birmingham Canal

1863
Albert Works Opens with
a
Turkish Bath!

Memorial plaque in the Jewellery Quarter

Graffiti in Hurst Street

The redeveloped Birmingham Central Library

Looking towards Chamberlain Square

Cambrian Wharf

City skyline

Spencer Street, Jewellery Quarter

The Malt House

Luxury apartments alongside Birmingham Canal

Birmingham city centre from the Jewellery Quarter

Hurst Street graffiti

EVERYTHING HAPPENS HERE
POLARBEAR & SIMON TURNER
COMMERCE AND LABOUR
WARMS THE WALLS
OF OUR CITY.
AND WILL DO AGAIN:
OF THE STREETS
THE MUSIC OF OUR MACHINE
AND ALTOGETHER.

The Water Wall near Bullring

burger